My Little Fireflies

Poems of Nostalgia and Everyday Magic

Rasika Raghunath

Made with ❤ on the BookLeaf Publishing Platform
www.bookleafpub.in
www.bookleafpub.com

Dedication

To my parents —

I'm forever grateful for the childhood you gave me, and for the lovely memories I return to on quiet days.

Preface

My Little Fireflies is a collection of poems inspired by my childhood — little moments that brought joy, wonder, and left a lasting mark on a small girl's heart. Whenever life feels heavy or the days get rough, I find myself drifting back to those simpler times. A scent, a sound, or just a quiet moment can spark a memory — and suddenly, I'm there again, reliving the feeling, the laughter, the magic.

Maybe you picked up this book during a tea break, looking for a smile or simply to fill a quiet moment. Whatever the reason, I hope these poems stir something within you — a forgotten memory, a familiar feeling, or the thought of someone who once meant the world to you.

In the rush of everyday life, we often overlook the little things. But looking back, it's those small moments that shape who we become. Here's to keeping that spark alive. Thank you for joining me on this walk down memory lane.

With love,
Rasika Raghunath

Acknowledgements

Before anything else, I want to take a moment to thank the people and places that made this book possible. Behind every page are memories, encouragement, and love — and I am deeply grateful to those who have supported me along the way.

To my family — I am deeply grateful to you for always standing by me with unwavering support.

To my husband — thank you for being my biggest cheerleader, for encouraging me to do my best, and for always inspiring me to aim higher.

To my readers — thank you for picking up this book. I hope it brings a smile to your face and a warm memory to your heart.

A heartfelt thank you to **BookLeaf Publishing** for this wonderful opportunity. This journey brought me back to poetry after many years. As a child, I loved to write, but somewhere along the way, that passion faded and self-doubt crept in. I'm deeply grateful for this experience, which helped me rekindle that love.

To my country, India — for your rich culture, timeless traditions, and everyday magic. From the scent of monsoons to the rhythm of temple bells, your beauty lives in every memory I've tried to capture here.

And finally, **to life itself** — for teaching me that even in the darkest moments, love will always find a way through.

1. My Little Fireflies

On gloomy days,
When the clouds are grey,
Or when the skies are clear,
But your heart feels the weight,

Close your eyes,
And take in the dark,
Wait for the light
To wave its path.

A flicker of light
Is seen afar.
Not too clear,
But it's coming near.

You take a deep breath,
Eyes still shut,
The flicker comes close,
With a familiar touch.

Little memories
From your past—
Childhood whispers
That forever last.

First comes one,
Followed by more,
Little hearts
That carry a part of your soul.

They fly around you,
Oh so quiet,
But deep inside,
You feel the light.

A small smile
Spreads on your face—
Soft and true,
A warm embrace.

The heart feels light,
You start to float,
Lifted by joy,
Each flicker wrote.

Voices, moments,
Senses from before,
A journey returns,
Flowing to your core.

These fireflies are your own,

Protecting you from the start—
Moments of joy
Stored deep in your heart.

Ready for a new day,
And new memories to store,

For anytime you
Feel low,
It's time for the fireflies' show.

2. Dandelions

So many flowers,
Bright as day,
Though the garden was full of charm,
One little flower
Caught her gaze.

Round little flowers,
Light as air,
White like a grandpa's beard—
Apoopan thadi,
Known in tales,
A hush of wonder,
In the air.

A whispering flower
That carries your dreams away.

She'd close her eyes,
Dream her wish,
And let it fly.

Too many dreams
For one little heart,
She wished again,

With a new start.

Every time the flowers came home,
The little girl would hold them close,
And hide them safe,
In her pencil box.

One box became two,
And slowly, when she had a wish,
She'd secretly take them out,
Whisper a dream,
And let the flower fly—

To lands far away,
Carrying her little wish,
Hoping it comes true one day.

Her magical *apoopan thadi*,
The flower that delivers your wish,
One day.

3. Before The Bus Came

The clock strikes six,
And a gentle knock falls on the door.
A small, annoyed grumble replies,
As the curtains are drawn away.

Dragging feet and a sleepy face—
"Eat quickly, or you'll be late," Amma says.

Shoes brushed at the last minute,
Ponytails in place,
She grabs everything in sight
And runs down the stairs.

Half past seven, the school bus arrives—
A bunch of loud hi's and an excited goodbye.

There she goes,
The start of a new day.
So many new stories to be told,
And so many to be made.

4. The Rain

Clouds turn grey,
And a distant thunder rumbles.
There's a shift in the wind,
And the smell of wet sand fills the air.

"Amma, look! It's raining!"
She ran outside.
"Don't get drenched,"
Yelled a voice from inside.

Her favourite *Poppy* umbrella in hand,
And a gleam of excitement in her eyes,
She looked up at the sky—
It was time to play.

It didn't matter if she was an only child,
Her imagination took centre stage,
And she found a friend
In the rain.

Splish, splash, she jumped in the puddles,
Whirling the umbrella,
Spraying the raindrops everywhere.

She danced to the left,
And to the right.
By now, her clothes were wet,
And the umbrella was nowhere in sight.

Out came the paper boats,
Racing upon the brook.
A thrill like no other,
A memory for life.

As it poured,
A hungry girl made her way
To a plate of hot fritters,
To end her day.

Her mother's hands,
Gentle and warm, towelled her hair
While she yapped away.
Rain and thunder played along—
Oh, what a beautiful day!

5. The Joy Of A Weekend

School was fun,
But nothing could match
The joy of a weekend.

Her day would begin
With her parents on either side,
Sitting on her bed,
Pulling her leg,
Laughter spilling like morning light.

They laughed together,
They ate together—
Such simple joys
In her little world.

Then off she would go,
On big adventures
With her little family:
Mom, Dad, and her.

Dressed in something new,
With accessories to match it all,
She sat in the backseat of the car,
While her favourite songs,

Played on the radio.

Mom chattered away,
While Dad chimed in,
And drove them everywhere.

She smiled when they laughed,
Wishing she could freeze the frame—
And not let time slip by.

Movie nights
With buttered popcorn and cream buns,
Or temple visits
With delicious sweets.

She found beauty
In the little things—
She could never pick a side.

She pictured the stories her parents shared,
Tearing into crisp *dosas* with her hands,
At a humble drive-thru,
Windows down,
Laughter spilling with every bite.

She loved long rides to the beach—
The smell of the sea,

The sound of the people,
The wind in her hair.

Her little world—
It was all there.

She shared her stories from school,
Dad offered his usual advice,
And Mom teased him with a grin.

It was never complete
Without a stop for ice cream.
So many flavours to choose from,
She could never decide.

Then they'd sit in the car,
Sundaes in hand,
Laughing between spoonfuls.
She'd look up at them—
And smile.

She didn't need anything more.
It was all there.

6. Time With Her Granddad

"Veliachaaa," she'd fondly call him,
Her maternal granddad.

She had the best grandparents,
But it was with him
She spent most of her growing years.

News blaring on full volume,
They'd bicker like kids,
But when the smell of fish curry
Floated from the kitchen,
They'd come together —
And thulp like there's no tomorrow.

He made the boring things
Not so boring.

He taught her to save,
To write cheques and letters—
Neat and formal was his way.

Just a schoolgirl,
Yet important she felt,
When he'd hand her paper and say,

"Write to the bank, will you?
My handwriting's not that great."

They went on little adventures
To the post office,
Learning things
That helped her when she grew up.

Birthdays were a big deal —
He'd insist on getting a card,
Slip neat little notes of cash inside,
And help with the décor,
Just to see her eyes light up.

Every *Ganesh Chaturthi,*
Hand in hand, they'd go
Through market lanes
In a festive glow.
She'd choose the idol,
Calm and sure,
While he, with knowing, smiling eyes,
Let her pick a toy she'd eyed before—
A little joy he could not ignore.

They'd go walking together,
Ending their day with roasted peanuts,
Or playing tennicoit and badminton.

"Veliachaaa," she'd call out,
Every time she had a story to tell.

He'd laugh until tears came,
Loving every bit
Of being a part of her little life.

"Veliachaaa," she'd call out.
He took a piece of her heart when he moved on,
But she was grateful —
So grateful —
For the memories they shared.

7. Friendship

Friendships so tender,
Friendships so pure,
Small actions
That leave a mark,
So wide.

They joked,
They played,
They jumped,
They ate.

It was chaos
To the outer world,
But oh, the joy
It left her with.

Then comes Friendship Day—
Oh, so dear in every way
To a schoolgirl back in the day,
A moment that would never stray.

The night before,
She'd sit up late,
Pick the ones

With beads and flowers,
And set them aside
For every friend.

She'd make a chart
With all their names,
The pretty ones
For the ones on top.

They'd exchange bands
And little notes.
Like a badge of honour,
They'd wear it all day.

Years later,
She found a little box—
Still inside were the bands she got.
Aged they seemed,
But the bond they shared
Still continued to live on.

Friendships,
That grew with time.

8. What's In The Box?

Hot hot food,
In her favourite bag,
She'd swing it side to side
On her way to school—zigzag!

When lunch break got close,
Her tummy would start rumbling.
She'd think of Amma's yummy food,
And smile while quietly mumbling—

"What's in the box today?" she'd wonder.

"Trinnnng!" went the bell!
She rushed to her bag,
Excited as well!

Open goes the lid—
Oh, what a surprise!
Flower-shaped *uthapams*
With smiley-faced eyes,
And animal-shaped ones on the side.

Tiny little *idlis*,
With ghee and *podi*,

Or *chapathi* rolls,
With all kinds of fillings!

Noodles too! Twisty and neat,
Made just right—her favourite treat.

Every day,
"What's in the box?" she'd wonder,
A tasty surprise.
But one thing stayed the same—
Amma's love,
The secret spice.

She'd wake up early,
Without a fuss,
To cook up magic,
Just for us.

And that's how the girl
Began to enjoy
The joy of food—
Throughout her life.

Even now, she still can't decide...
What's for lunch? Or what's on the side?
What would Amma make, if she was by my side?

9. My Little Tooth Fairy

One little baby tooth,
Shakes its little legs.
Turns to the right,
And turns to the left.

She plays with her tongue,
And wiggles it around.

The tooth puts up a fight,
Not ready to come out.

Then, with a towel,
She gives a gentle pull—
Pop! It's free.

She runs to Dad,
And Mom smiles,
For the fairy, it's set aside.

Night arrives,
She wishes on the tooth,
And says goodbye.
She tucks it beneath her pillow.
A little letter rests by its side.

Sunrise comes,
She quickly checks—
The tooth is gone,
The fairy's gift now gleams!

Happy as ever,
She takes her note,
And off it goes,
Sliding into her little piggy bank.

10. Train Rides

Summer vacation arrived,
And it was time for her train ride.

She'd pack her little bag,
With food neatly tucked inside.

Checklists were run,
And off they'd go.

Station it is—
Familiar sounds and voices loud,
She'd see people pacing around.

She spots the musical weighing scale,
From far away.
"Amma, please. Just one coin," she'd claim—

Down goes the coin,
And the machine comes awake,
A little card slips out,
Telling a fortune
In a magical way.
A little ritual,
Always the same.

So many people,
Busy with their lives—
She'd observe them all
While sitting on her suitcase.

She spots her cousin,
Waving from afar.
There she runs,
To greet them with a hi.

The announcement's made,
And the train arrives.
They quickly grab their bags
And run to the train,
Searching for their names
On a white, pale list.

A quick jump and off they go,
Looking for the numbers
Marked for them to know.

She climbs up
To the upper berth,
Her cousin beside her.
Loud as ever,
They'd play their games,

While the elders talked
Down below.

The train picks up speed and zooms by,
Windows rattle and their stomachs grumble.

From sandwiches to idlis,
They'd have it all—
Neatly packed in foil and love.

But still, when the train halts,
The smell of omelettes floats by.
They'd want it all—
In vain they'd whine.

A cloth is tied
Between the berths,
So no one slips—
Everything secure.

Between the games
And stories told,
Somewhere along the ride,
She drifts away—

A content sleep,
Before their station arrives.

11. The World Of Books

Ah, the smell of books—
Old and new,
Stories tucked in,
In a world she never knew.

From her stack so high,
She'd pick one that caught her eye,
Hold it close and find her spot—
Off she goes,
Deep into the plot.

She swam through seas,
Ran through fields,
Fought the beasts,
And danced to beats.

The windows took her
To a world of magic,
A world of adventure,
A world of charm.
Every day,
Drifting to a different place.

Books taught her love,

Taught her empathy,
Opened colourful doors
To a world of emotions.

Different stories,
Different perspectives—
She could never put one down
Until the very end.

Even past bedtime, she'd quietly stay,
One lamp glowing, story at play.
A blanket, a pillow, tucked just right,
Forgetting there's school with dawn in sight.

She'd read till the end,
Then close her eyes,
Letting the story
Softly rewind.

Ah, that feeling, fresh and true,
When a story ends—
And you feel brand new.

She lived in dreams
both wild and true,
A space her heart kept wandering to.

12. Just Like Her Dad

Two little kids
Sat across the table—
One in his 40s,
One in her teens.

Fingers tapped like tabla beats
On the glass-top table,
Eyes gleaming,
Mischief in the air.

Breakfast done,
Amma walks in, with her magic dish—
Banana, warm and caramel sweet.
Two pairs of eyes meet,
And off they jump
To grab the best pieces.

"Amma, look! He's taking my share!"
She'd yell.
Dad would laugh
And tease,
"Oh, too late. That was the best piece!"

She'd whine and grab the plate—

Off she goes,
Her dad behind her.

She'd run to the right,
He'd leap to the left—
A whole bunch of shouting,
A whole lot of squealing.
Amma would exclaim,
"It's like two kids in the house!"

But that's what happens
When the girl
Takes after her dad—
Two big foodies
Fighting for treats,
Because nothing comes close
To Amma's tasty feasts!

13. When The Music Finds Her

Door closed,
Walkman in hand,
Her favourite tape
Tucked safely inside.

A soft click,
A scratchy hiss,
Before the music starts to play.

She fixes her earphones,
Shuts her eyes—
And slowly, the world slips away.

The beat picks up,
The words begin to pour.

Her hands start to sway,
Her feet tap away,
Barefoot,
To a song only she can hear.

She drifts into a world,
Where every word

Speaks to her.

She feels like a star,
With the spotlight on,
Standing tall,
Alone in the glow of the stage.

There's something about dancing,
With her eyes closed—
A joy unfolds.

Suddenly, life feels lighter,
And the little girl
Fades into the moment.

When the beats go up,
Her hair comes loose,
When the music slows,
Out comes the grace.

There's rhythm to her steps,
And she laughs,
When she loses her balance
Spinning around.

The music comes to an end,
Her eyes slowly open—

She sees herself in the mirror—
A gentle smile—
And maybe—just maybe—
The world feels new again.

14. A Day Full Of Magic

With school the next day,
She's told to sleep early, tucked away.
She drifts into dreams,
When a whisper floats through the night.

She tiptoes softly to her door,
Presses her ear against the floor.
A bunch of voices, soft and light,
Excited in the middle of the night.

"Shushhh! It's her birthday!" someone says.
A secret smile grows across her face.
She tiptoes back, heart beating fast,
Slips beneath the sheet,
Hugs her pillow tight,
And drifts back to sleep.

Morning breaks with cheers and laughter.
She runs into the living room,
Where streamers hang,
And balloons bob in the air.

"Happy Birthday!" they shout,
Hugs and kisses tumble all around.

Favourite breakfast on the table,
And neatly packed gifts in the corner,
Cards opened with careful hands.

School flies by,
With chocolates distributed,
And the party awaits
Back at home.
Friends come running in,
Parents chatting by the side.

Games in every corner,
A ball rolling across the floor,
Little feet racing past,
Voices ringing in every room.

A creative cake, a child's dream,
Sits waiting at the center.
She hops toward it,
In her brand new dress.

Songs are sung,
Candles are blown,
The cake is cut,
Laughter fills the room.

When night falls and all is quiet,

Her friends head home,
Waving a little bag
Full of goodies and smiles.

With a heart full of joy,
And a grateful smile,
She thanks her family,
And tucks away—
Such magic, and a perfect day.

15. Vishu, Through Her Eyes

April whispers—
Vishu is near,
The start of a new year,
Warm and clear.

She runs to bed
Before the clock strikes twelve,
For she's been told—
Eyes must wake
To golden light.

At dawn, her mother
Tiptoes in,
Whispers a wish,
With a sleepy grin.

Eyes closed tight,
Hand in hand,
They make their way
Down the stairs.

Lids flutter open—
A golden world aglow,
A smiling idol,

Decked with gold.

Coins that glint,
Jewels that gleam,
A *valkannadi*
Catches her dream.

Yellow blossoms with delicate stems,
Fruits and veggies,
Arranged with care,
Tiny brass lamps,
Polished to shine.

She bows her head,
Makes her wish,
Receives a note,
With a coin or two,
Tucked away
Like something new.

Back to bed
Off she runs,
Heart still glowing
From the lamps,
Like the rising sun.

Morning calls,

Off she goes,
In new clothes bright,
To temple steps,
And family homes—
With cousins all around.

A grand feast awaits—
She eats with pride,
Payasam warm
And joy inside.

And when it's done,
Her belly full and tight,
Her piggy bank full
And a happy sight.

Curtains drawn,
Dreams in flight—
Vishu rests
In golden light.

16. It's Time!

Vacation's almost done,
Memories stay—
A brand new year
Is on its way.

One week left,
Prep time's here:
Uniforms pressed,
New shoes appear.

Then comes shopping,
Her favorite part—
A bag, some pencils,
A lunchbox with heart.

Floral *Apsara* pencils,
Shaped sharpeners too,
Scented erasers
In pink and blue.

A pencil box
With built-in games,
A zip that sings
As she packs her things.

She lines them up,
Her perfect set,
In matching shades—
Her best one yet.

Out come the books,
Wrapped in brown,
New labels neat
With her name written down.

She smells the pages,
Tucks them in tight,
Heart all set
For her first day bright.

A new teacher, a new class,
A brand new space,
Friends old
And friends new,
With a heart full of dreams—
She's all set to go.

17. Amma's Stories

Evening light, soft and low,
Curtains dancing, a golden glow.
Pillows puffed and set just right,
She'd curl up in Amma's lap each night.

She closed her eyes
As Amma began—
Her voice gentle, steady, and warm.
As her hand grazed through the girl's hair,
She'd weave each tale with tender charm.

Pictures bloomed,
Characters unfolded,
A gentle music played,
As the story came to life.

A fox's trick, a hungry bear,
A roach's trip, a dragonfly's flight,
A king's brave quest,
Or tales from Amma's younger days—
The stories changed with each twilight.

Her world would move
Like magic in the air,

Myths whispered
As if they'd happened there.

Like whispers and thunders,
Her voice rose and fell—
She listened closely, her mind held still—
The stories had a magic will.

No movies, no screens,
No dazzling shows,
Just Amma's words
In a gentle flow.

A kiss placed soft on her head,
The story done, she'd whisper goodnight,
Adjust the sheets,
And tiptoe out with a smile.

Lights turned off,
The door closed,
The girl would drift—
Still in the tale,
Until morning light.

18. Bharatanatyam

Short hair falling next to her ears,
Cute half ponytail in place,
Dressed in simple green and red,
With a thin red band tied at the waist.

Holding Amma's hand,
She made her way
To the next street,
Where dancers moved in grace.

She was merely five
When she stepped inside.
But oh,
It was love at first sight.

The *raagas, thaalam,*
And the musical chimes of the *salangai*
Flew her to a different age.

Baby steps, to the right and left—
Patiently she learnt,
While her guru smiled.

With time, the steps began to speak—

Of love, of loss, of battles grand.
She found her joy
In tales that danced
Upon the land.

Stories and emotions
Paving their way,
She took the form
Of the character
As she swayed.

Such was the beauty
Of this ancient art divine –
No two days danced the same,
Each moment marked in time.

From basic *adavus*, slow and sure
To tales from the past gracefully told,
She glided along—
Her stories fierce, her gestures bold.

A god, a queen, a lover, a sage,
Nature's beauty or a deer making its way,
Her body moved to the story's script,
A storyteller that fills the space.

Then came the day

The curtains rose,
A sacred space,
The stage aglow.

In colours bright,
With kohl-lined eyes,
She stepped ahead,
Her spirits high.

Alta painted, palms and feet,
Jewels shimmered,
With *salangai* tied, ready for flight.

And so began the tale she wove,
As she swayed,
Capturing the audience—
It was love, once again.

19. Little Letters Of Love

A little girl, with hands so small,
Made cards for loved ones,
One and all.

With paper, pens, and stickers too,
Hearts and glitter,
All bright and new.

Colourful crayons joined the fun,
Stick-figure drawings, a happy sun.
Her words wobbly, ran across the page,
Love was there, soft and bubbly, at every stage.

Edges cut,
Ribbons tied,
A secret treasure,
Tucked inside.

The night before,
She'd work so late,
Making cards for every special date.

Morning arrives—
Eyes wide,

She runs to them,
With a smile so bright.
She'd give the card and watch their delight.

They'd beam with joy
And hug her tight,
"This made my day!"
"Oh! What a sight!"
"The best one yet!" they'd proudly say,
"I wouldn't have it any other way!"

20. Annual Day Is Here!

The best part of school,
Without a doubt,
Is when *Annual Day* comes about.

A month ahead, the buzz begins,
With trials, practices, and hopeful grins.

She beams with joy,
Her hand held high,
Eager to dance,
Never shy.

Every year, she takes the chance,
Skits at times, but mostly dance.

Zero hour, they say,
As practice sets sail each day.
Groups are formed with pride and cheer,
As the big day draws ever near.

Songs are chosen,
Steps are set,
Teachers guiding,
Energy met.

Formations are made,
Movements refined,
Everyone making sure,
Everything is aligned.

Amidst the rhythm and the song,
New friendships bloom, growing strong.
An hour each day to laugh and play,
As they prepare for the grand display.

Costumes ready, instructions clear,
Rehearsals bloom as the show draws near.
The hall across the street stands tall,
Awaiting songs and roaring call.

The day arrives— excitement in the air,
Families gather, like a fair.
Rooms abuzz with final prep,
Makeup, hair, run through every step.

"One, two, three, cheese!" — photos snapped,
Groups captured, memories wrapped.

Then hush descends, the moment starts,
The music plays, with pounding hearts.
In line they move, nervous smiles,

They see the crowd— their spirits fly.

Curtains open, the volume is set high,
She steps on stage, lights shining bright,
Crowd unseen, heart feels light.

Music flows, she finds her pace,
Lost in dance, a joyful grace.

Each movement sure, each turn precise,
In that moment — pure paradise.

As the song slows, a final pose,
Thunderous applause, the curtains close.

Backstage chatter, excited much,
Compliments shared, faces bright.

Parents arrive with hugs and praise,
Celebrating these golden days.

Costumes off, stories retold,
Laughter shared, memories gold.

Off they go to feast and cheer,
To celebrate their grand show.

21. What Is Love?

What is love? she wondered.

Maybe it's the teary goodbyes,
And hugs you see at the airport.

Or stumbling upon handwritten letters,
That speak of a different time.

What is love? she wondered.

Maybe it's your mom
Saving the last piece of your favourite food for you.

Or when a puppy
Comes and rubs their nose
On your face.

What is love? she wondered.

Maybe it's when you see an old couple,
Laughing and enjoying their time.

The flowers at your doorstep,
Or the box of cookies

That reminded them of you.

What is love? she wondered.

The time when you glanced back
At the mirror and smiled at yourself—
A little kindness that your heart couldn't deny.

What is love? she wondered.

Was it the time your friend
Gave you her favourite eraser
Because you lost yours?

Or when your dad got you that toy you liked,
Even though money was tight?

Was it the long phone calls,
Or the goofy smiles?

What is love? she wondered.
She couldn't decide.

Maybe it's the little texts you get
Just to check on you.

Or the quiet foot massage

At the end of a long day.

What is love? she wondered.

The embraces, the smiles,
The food, the tears,
The books, the notes,
The pictures, the dates.

She really couldn't decide.

What is love? she wondered.

A gentle breeze touched her,
And she looked up at the sky—
So many stars,
All shining bright.

That's when it hit her.
Love shows up in different disguises.
It's infinite.

Love stirs the heart,
And helps you survive.

22. Sticky Fingers!

School is done,
We tumble out, one by one,
Huddled in groups near the gate,
Stomachs grumbling — we can't wait!

The smell of street food floats our way,
Mangoes cut with chilli spray.
Fruits in flower shapes so neat,
A colourful, afternoon treat.

Tiny *samosas*, perfect and hot,
In queue we wait —
Sometimes, no luck.

Pink clouds of cotton candy,
Sticky fingers, it is,
A cart rolls by,
A sugary win.

A glass box filled with snowy delight,
An old man smiles,
With *soan papdi* in sight.

Opposite the gate,

Off we run,
When time is more,
For chocolate tubes — one, two, a ton!
We tear them open, suck them slow,
Sticky grins begin to show.

If summer is here,
We hear the bells from afar —
The ice cream cart arrives,
With Choco Bars for the heart.

Coins clutched tight in hand,
We rush like wind,
To not miss our chance.

And then we walk,
Stomachs content,
While we wait
For our school van.

23. Off We Go!

Once a year—
No books to pack, no homework due,
A bag so light, with snacks and juice,
Adventure calls, and hearts feel new.

Dropped off early, a buzzing scene,
Name lists, teachers, and friends between.
Laughter rising, eyes so bright,
An exciting journey now in sight.

They board the bus with waving smiles,
Ready to roll for fun-filled miles.
Music plays, and spirits soar,
A sing-along starts, they ask for more.

The bus comes alive with cheerful delight,
They jump, they dance, they play, they fight.
Just like that, it's been an hour,
As the gates arrive—today's the day!

Sometimes it's the zoo—
Where lions roar and parrots squawk,
They point at monkeys, giggle and talk,
Call each other names and run about,

Full of wonder, full of shout!

Sometimes it's the planetarium,
Where they sit wide-eyed in the dark,
Staring at stars and glowing rings,
Gasping each time there's a spark.

Or a resort with wide green lawns,
Where slides await and music plays,
They run and tumble, laugh and cheer—
A truly unforgettable day.

Welcome drinks wait in various trays,
Buffet waiting in the halls inside.
Bags set down, and off they race—
Games and dance take up the space.

Teachers join in, carefree and bright,
Everyone soaked in joy and light.
Photos clicked, poses made,
Tug-of-war happening under the shade.

The sun dips low, the day winds back,
Time to trace their way back on track.
Some doze off, their energy spent,
Some still swaying to the beats at play.

As the school gates come in view,
Parents wait with eager eyes too.
Doors open, and off they fly—
Cheers, hi-fives, and loving embrace nearby.

Stories tumble, wide and fast,
Of a day too perfect to ever pass.

24. The Games We Played

Simpler times,
When new games were made
Every two days.

With friends or cousins,
Imagination was the main player.

Sometimes *house house*,
Sometimes ghost,
Sometimes doctor,
And sometimes cook—
They'd find things in the house,
Pretending to be someone new.

Hours would fly
As they ran round the block,
Games on the road—
Stones thrown,
Chalk-drawn squares,
Balls in the air,
Or hide and seek behind pillars.

Fun, loud, hyper,
Running out of breath—

They'd never stop
Till parents called their names out.

A new day,
A new set,
New rules,
New players,
New games.

25. A Day By The Sea

Waves crash, loud and wild,
The scent of wet sand fills the air.
Bells ring in the distance—
Carts clatter,
Voices rise,
A hum of joy everywhere.

She walks barefoot on golden ground,
Feet sinking slowly,
Shells and sand weaving
Between her toes.

Toward the waves she runs,
A gleam in her eye,
Excitement dancing
In every stride.

When the water meets her skin,
It hits—
Cold and sudden,
Her heart skips,
But joy unfolds.

With every wave,

Her dress feels heavy,
But her heart feels light.

A few more chases with the tide,
Then she turns—
To stalls where colours call.

Balloons lined up,
Ready to pop,
Horses trotting,
Carousels spinning
To tunes that never stop.

She draws her name in the sand—
Letters soft,
Then swiped away,
A quiet magic in the air.

Hot peanuts in hand,
Salt on her skin,
Voices of birds
And waves rolling in.

Families scattered,
Kids running through,
The simple life—
Like they know it too.

And when it's time,
Her parents call her name—
One last glance,
One last inhale,
Before she goes,
Back home,
Carrying the calm of the waves within.

26. A Shopper's Delight!

She jumped into an auto,
With Amma by her side—
A sparkle in their morning,
Adventure in their stride.

Through bustling lanes,
Where bazaar stalls rise,
Earrings shimmered,
Like stars in disguise.

Racks of colours, bold and bright,
Polka dots, frills, and lace so light.
Pastels soft, and shades darker than the night,
They wandered on, hearts feather-light.

Tops or skirts,
Dresses or shoes,
Jewellery or accessories—
She never could choose.

Bargain after bargain,
Mom's purse grew light,
And their bags brimmed
With delight.

A snack, a sip, a moment to rest,
Then home they went, their hearts full,
Blessed.

With joy, she waited—
Ears tuned to the car's soft hum,
A turn in the lane,
The moment had come.

She twirled in each dress,
A wave in the air,
Compliments followed—
"A fashion show!" they'd declare.

And with the last cheer,
She got ready for the night.
She drifted asleep,
Dreaming of wearing each dress with pride.

27. Assembly Days

Twice a week we'd make our way
Down the steps in bright array,
Sunlight warming every line—
Tiny girls in perfect time.

Ribbons in place,
Shoes shining white,
With chalk in hand,
We'd get them right.

"One arm's distance!" came the shout,
Noisy whispers sorted out.
First, the prayer, soft and slow,
Then news and thoughts we'd proudly show.

The birthday song in chorus rang,
As girls in new frocks shyly stood,
A smiling *"thank you"* barely said,
In front of all, yet understood.

And sometimes came the loudest cheer,
When house points were announced clear—
A sudden uproar, claps, and cries,
With victory shining in their eyes.

The pledge was told,
With heads held high,
The national anthem sung
With steady pride.

Some days it stretched a little long,
And someone'd drop down with a sigh—
Just a trick we all could tell,
The nearby giggles drifting by.

When it was time to walk away,
Back to class from the start of day,
PT teachers stood with gaze—
Nails and collars met their praise.

But if we strayed or broke the line,
A quick run around would do just fine.
Still, we walked in sun's sweet rays,
With stories tucked from assembly days.

28. Ohh! The Exams Are Here!

Exams approaching,
Studies in full swing—
Extra classes, notes,
Revisions begin.

Tempers fly,
Tears sometimes shed,
Some days a breeze,
With confidence instead.

The night before,
An energy from somewhere—
She learns more,
Her speed picks up midair.

Then the day arrives,
And chaos sets—
A stillness lingers
In the air it nets.

Parents wish her luck,
A stop at the temple,
Books wrapped neat,

Writing pad and pens assembled.

Uniforms crisp,
One last check made,
Before she heads to school—
Like any other day.

She arrives to a quiet air,
Solemn faces everywhere,
Whispers float across the space,
Friends huddle in their last-minute race.

One explains, one tries to guess,
Mentors for a moment—
In the pre-exam phase.

Suddenly, the bell rings loud,
"It's time", they say,
Bags outside,
Just essentials in play.

Benches lined,
Roll numbers marked—
She finds her seat,
And waits, heart sparked.

Teacher walks in,

Serious and straight,
A soft *"Good morning,"*
Then the prayer plays.

Question papers are handed out,
With empty sheets to fill—
The bell rings again—
It's time to test the will.

She scans the page,
Familiar questions smile,
A tricky one here and there—
She saves it for a while.

Time ticks on,
Sometimes slow, sometimes fast—
It all depends
On the questions asked.

She raises her hand
For an extra sheet,
Friends glance over—
A teasing awaits.

She grins, knowing well
What's coming next—
The joke's on the ground

At her writing text.

The teacher strolls,
Quiet and alert,
Silence broken only
By pencils sharpened.

"Time's almost up,"
The teacher says—
Threads are passed
To tie the essays.

If time remains,
She doodles in the question paper,
Checks her details,
Signs things properly.

The bell rings again,
And papers go in—
They rush outside
With relieved grins.

Parents waiting
With eager eyes
To know how it went—
And then, a relieved sigh.

"One down!" someone cheers,
As they all reappear—

Off to the shop
For a chocolate cheer.

29. Ready, Set, Stage!

Her hand would go up
For every competition they'd call—
Enthusiastic as ever,
Confidence at its peak.

Solo or group,
She didn't mind,
She just loved getting prepped
And standing before the mic.

Recitations, elocutions,
Drama, music,
Dance—always.
Fashion shows at times,
Mime, art,
Sports even.

In school or outside,
Her name would be there.

Her mother would guide her through—
Be it fancy dress
Or project displays.
She'd work on the props,

And the costumes too,
Then train the little girl
To speak just right,
Or make the perfect move.

"Have fun," she'd say,
"And most of all, if you forget—
Smile and make something up!
They won't know
What you prepared."

Off she'd go,
Happy and thrilled—
Sometimes a win,
Sometimes a loss.
But it didn't really matter—
It was the experience, after all.

30. The World Through Her Eyes

Carefree, yet feeling every shade,
She watches more than she says.
Little in size,
But don't be fooled—
Her heart runs deep,
And her world is full.

She sees whimsical clouds
That turn into animals,
Raindrops catching light,
Reflections swirling within.

Rainbows stretch across the sky—
She wonders softly,
"Where do they end?"

Thunder and lightning—
"A wedding in the skies," she's told.
She smiles at the story,
Tucks it in her soul.

Crowds on the street,
So many lives—

She imagines their stories,
Their dreams, their drives.

She sees women
Striding with grace,
Talking and laughing—
She wonders,
"Will I be like that someday?"

She sees her mother
Cooking without a guide,
A pinch of this,
A swirl of that—
She wonders if one day
She'd hold that kind of magic too.

She sees her dad
Tallying notes
And balancing books,
Precise and steady—
She wonders if she'd ever
Be that organised too.

She sees her grandmothers—
One serene like early dawn,
The other stirring sweetness
Into every festive treat.

She wonders how they were
When they were little girls too—
Running through courtyards
With anklets and cotton frocks.

She sees her grandfathers—
One brimming with stories
And cheer that never tires,
The other, quiet,
Savoring fish curry
And the rustle of newspapers.
She wonders if she walks like one,
And dreams of the days
When the other lived abroad,
His tales tucked in letters and smiles.

She sees the cat purr,
The dog softly rolls,
And wonders—
"What if they spoke back to her?"

A young couple
Walks by, hands held tight—
She wonders
If love would one day
Feel that light.

A plane flies above—
Tiny in the blue.
She dreams of the memories
And the stories they'd get,
From places so new.

She'd see half-demolished houses,
With tiles peeled off,
But a small mirror intact—
And wonder the life
And magic it held.

Kolams drawn in temple lanes,
White on red, like gentle stains.
She dreams of a time
Before she was born,
A world different,
Now reborn.

She sees it all—
But doesn't always speak.
It sits in her heart,
Layered and deep.

The urge to help,
The urge to smile,
To ask, to listen,

To dream a while—
To live it all
In her own quiet style.

So if you've ever watched the clouds,
Or listened more than you spoke—
If you've felt the world
In quiet ways,
You've carried those fireflies too.
Somewhere deep inside,
They're still glowing.

My little fireflies—
Are yours too.